THE MAGICAL STORY CHEST

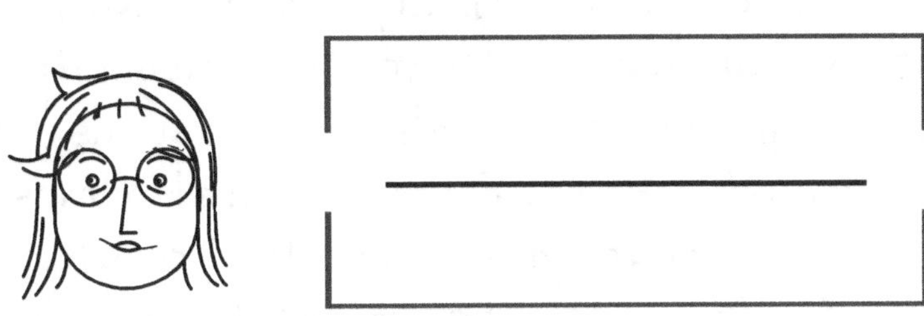

A Collection of Enchanting Adventures"

"The Magical Story Chest: A Collection of Enchanting Adventures" is a captivating anthology that opens the door to a world brimming with wonder and enchantment. Within its pages lies a treasure trove of imaginative tales, carefully crafted to ignite the imaginations of young readers. Each story unfurls like a mystical journey, whisking children away to far-off lands, introducing them too endearing characters, and immersing them in extraordinary quests. From whimsical creatures and spellbinding quests to unexpected friendships and heartwarming lessons, this collection of enchanting adventures serves as a gateway to limitless possibilities. Every turn of the page unlocks the magic within, nurturing a love for reading and sparking dreams that will last a lifetime.

Step into a world where dreams take flight and imagination knows no bounds. Welcome to "The Magical Story Chest: A Collection of Enchanting Adventures," a literary treasure trove that beckons young readers on a mesmerizing journey through realms teeming with wonder and delight.

Within the pages of this enchanting anthology, a multitude of extraordinary tales awaits, each carefully curated to ignite the imaginations of children and transport them to realms beyond their wildest dreams. From the first glimpse, the velvety cover adorned with mystical creatures and twinkling stars, to the moment the chest is unlocked, a sense of anticipation fills the air.

As the lid swings open, a symphony of words spills forth, revealing a tapestry of whimsical creatures, courageous heroes, and magical lands. These stories weave a spell that captures the hearts of young and old alike, blending fantastical adventures with valuable life lessons. From the towering peaks of mountains draped in clouds to hidden forest glens echoing with laughter, every tale offers a portal into a world where anything is possible.

"The Magical Story Chest" holds the key to unlocking a love for reading, nourishing young minds and nurturing a lifelong passion for storytelling. So, dear reader, embark on this enchanting voyage and let your imagination soar amidst these wondrous pages.

The Magical Umbrella Adventure

Once upon a time, a young girl named Lily lived in a small community that was perched at the base of a majestic mountain.

Lily was known for her curious nature and boundless imagination. One rainy day, as she gazed out of her window, she noticed an old, tattered umbrella sitting in the corner of her room. Something about it seemed different, almost magical.

Unable to resist her curiosity, Lily picked up the umbrella and opened it. To her astonishment, the umbrella lifted her off the ground and began to soar through the rainy skies. Excitement filled her heart as she realized she was embarking on a grand adventure.

The magical umbrella carried Lily through billowing clouds, over vast meadows, and across sparkling rivers. She flew higher and higher until she reached a land she had only dreamed of—a land where animals talked and trees danced.

As she descended, the umbrella gently landed in a lush forest clearing. Surrounding her were friendly creatures of all shapes and sizes. There was Chester, the wise old owl with spectacles perched on his beak, and Berry, the mischievous squirrel with a twinkle in his eye. Lily quickly became friends with all the forest animals, who were thrilled to have a visitor from the human world.

Together, they embarked on a quest to find the legendary Crystal Lake, said to possess the power to grant wishes. Guided by Chester's knowledge of the land, they journeyed through magical meadows, crossed treacherous bridges, and braved mysterious caves.

Along the way, they encountered challenges that tested their bravery and friendship. Lily faced her fears as she crossed a rickety wooden bridge suspended high above a roaring waterfall. Berry used his nimble paws to unlock a hidden door, revealing a secret passage. And Chester's wisdom guided them through the darkest tunnels, where glow-in-the-dark mushrooms lit their path.

Finally, after days of adventure, they stood before the glistening Crystal Lake. Lily closed her eyes, made a wish with all her heart, and tossed a magical pebble into the shimmering waters. In an instant, her wish came true—a shower of colorful stars filled the sky, lighting up the forest in a dazzling display of magic and wonder.

With their mission accomplished, Lily bid a tearful farewell to her newfound friends. As she boarded the umbrella to return home, she promised to visit them again someday. The umbrella gracefully lifted her into the sky, carrying her back to her village.

From that day forward, Lily's imagination soared higher than ever before. She would often look at the old umbrella in the corner of her room, knowing that with a single wish, it could whisk her away on another extraordinary adventure. And so, with a heart full of memories and dreams, Lily eagerly awaited the next magical tale that awaited her.

The Brave Little Seedling

In a small garden nestled in the heart of a bustling city, there lived a brave little seedling named Sam. Sam was unlike any other seedling in the garden. While the others were content to stay rooted in the safety of the soil, Sam dreamed of exploring the world beyond the garden walls.

Every day, as the sun's warm rays embraced the garden, Sam would stretch upward, yearning to see what lay beyond the tall fence. The wind whispered stories of vast forests, rolling meadows, and majestic mountains. Sam's heart filled with curiosity and an unyielding desire for adventure.

One stormy night, as raindrops fell gently on the garden, Sam's chance for exploration arrived. A strong gust of wind blew open the garden gate, and Sam has swept away into the unknown.

The journey was perilous, but Sam's determination never wavered. Through rain and wind, Sam pushed forward, fueled by the dream of discovering a world beyond imagination.

Along the way, Sam met a wise old tree that shared stories of strength and resilience. The tree taught Sam about weathering the storms of life, and standing tall even when faced with adversity.

As days turned into weeks, Sam encountered numerous obstacles. Swarms of hungry insects, scorching sunrays, and parched landscapes challenged Sam's resolve. But the brave little seedling persisted, drawing strength from deep within.

One day, as the sun began its descent behind a magnificent mountain range, Sam arrived at a breathtaking meadow filled with vibrant wildflowers. The air was filled with the sweet scent of blooming blossoms, and a gentle breeze whispered tales of triumph and beauty.

In this meadow, Sam met a group of kind-hearted creatures—a butterfly, a ladybug, and a hummingbird. They were enchanted by Sam's resilience and bravery. Together, they danced among the flowers, sharing stories and laughter beneath the moonlit sky.

News of Sam's incredible journey spread throughout the meadow, inspiring other seedlings to seek their own adventures. Sam's courage had sparked a newfound sense of wonder and exploration among all the garden's inhabitants.

Filled with a sense of accomplishment and a heart bursting with joy, Sam decided it was time to return to the garden. With the help of the wind, Sam soared gracefully through the night sky, carrying stories of bravery and tales of growth.

Upon returning, Sam was greeted with open arms by the other seedlings, who marvelled at the extraordinary adventure. Sam's courageous spirit had transformed the once-ordinary garden into a place of dreams and limitless possibilities.

From that day forward, the garden flourished with the bravery and determination of every seedling.

Sam's story became a legend, passed down through generations, reminding them all that even the smallest among them could accomplish great feats. And so, the garden bloomed not only with vibrant flowers but also with the courage and resilience that had been inspired by the brave little seedling, Sam.

The Secret Door to Fairyland

In a quiet cottage nestled at the edge of a mystical forest, a young girl named Emily discovered an extraordinary secret. While exploring her grandmother's attic one sunny afternoon, she stumbled upon an old key hidden amidst a collection of forgotten treasures.

Intrigued by the key's ornate design and the mystery it held, Emily embarked on a quest to uncover its purpose. She scoured every nook and cranny of the cottage until she found a small, inconspicuous door tucked away behind a bookshelf.

With a gentle turn of the key, the door creaked open, revealing a magical world beyond her wildest dreams—Fairyland. Lush green meadows stretched as far as the eye could see, dotted with colorful flowers and shimmering streams. Tiny fairies flitted through the air, their delicate wings glistening in the sunlight.

Eager to explore this enchanting realm, Emily stepped through the secret door, leaving behind the ordinary world and entering a place filled with wonder and magic. The fairies greeted her with twinkling smiles, guiding her along a path that led to their ethereal kingdom.

The kingdom of the fairies was a breathtaking sight. Sparkling crystal castles stood tall, nestled among ancient trees adorned with luminescent leaves. Each step revealed a new delight—dancing waterfalls, talking animals, and mischievous pixies who giggled mischievously as they darted through the woods.

Emily's heart swelled with joy as she joined the fairies in their whimsical activities. She learned to weave delicate flower crowns, helped paint rainbows in the sky, and even befriended a kind-hearted unicorn named Stardust.

But Fairyland was not just a realm of blissful magic. It was a place where courage and kindness held great power. The fairies faced challenges of their own—a wicked sorceress who sought to extinguish the light of Fairyland with her dark magic.

Together with her newfound fairy friends, Emily embarked on a quest to confront the sorceress. They journeyed through treacherous forests and crossed trepidatious bridges, using their wits and bravery to overcome each obstacle.

In the heart of the sorceress's lair, Emily discovered a hidden source of light—a glowing crystal that radiated love and goodness. With her unwavering determination, Emily harnessed the power of the crystal, dispelling the sorceress's darkness and restoring harmony to Fairyland.

The fairies rejoiced, their wings fluttering in a symphony of joy. Emily bid farewell to her fairy friends, promising to return one day. Through the secret door, she stepped back into her grandmother's attic, clutching the key and a heart full of magical memories.

From that day forward, Emily treasured the secret door, knowing that whenever she craved adventure and wonder, Fairyland would always be just a key turn away. And in her ordinary world, she carried the lessons of courage, kindness, and the boundless magic that exists within the realms of imagination.

The Mischievous Talking Animals

An amazing event was happening in a small community tucked between undulating hills and bubbling streams. The villagers' animals had learned to speak, giving them a special talent.

It all started one fateful morning when a bright shooting star streaked across the sky, showering the village with magical stardust. Overnight, the once-silent creatures gained the power of speech. Word of this enchanting event spread quickly, and soon the village buzzed with excitement.

Among the mischievous talking animals were Benny the chatty squirrel, Lucy the wise old owl, and Max the playful fox. They quickly formed an unlikely trio and set out on adventures that were previously unimaginable.

The trio's first escapade took them to the bustling farmer's market. Hiding behind crates of ripe, juicy apples, Benny listened intently to the humans' conversations, picking up secrets and snippets of village gossip.

He would then relay the juicy tidbits to Lucy and Max, who would spread the news to their fellow animals. The village was abuzz with animal chatter, much to the surprise and amusement of the villagers.

But as time passed, the animals realized that their newfound ability came with great responsibility. They understood that they had the power to bridge the gap between humans and animals, fostering understanding and empathy.

With this in mind, Benny, Lucy, and Max organized a grand meeting at the village square, inviting humans and animals alike to share their stories and concerns. The once-separate worlds merged as villagers gathered, eager to listen to the tales of their furry and feathered neighbours.

The animals spoke of their struggles, their love for their homes, and the importance of living in harmony with nature. They shared their worries about disappearing habitats and the need for compassion towards all living beings.

The humans, in turn, expressed their gratitude for the animals' wisdom and vowed to protect their natural habitats.

From that day forward, the village transformed into a community that nurtured and respected all creatures. Humans and animals worked together to create safe havens for wildlife, planting trees and building shelters. They organized festivals celebrating the bond between humans and animals, where conversations flowed freely between species.

Benny, Lucy, and Max became beloved figures, bridging the divide between humans and animals with their mischievous antics and heartwarming stories. They were admired for reminding everyone that every creature, no matter how small, had a voice worth listening to.

As years went by, the magical stardust faded, and the animals returned to their silent ways. But the bond forged during those enchanted days remained unbreakable. The village thrived as a symbol of unity, where the mischievous talking animals were fondly remembered in legends and passed down from one generation to the next.

And though the animals could no longer speak, their legacy lived on, reminding all who listened that sometimes the most magical connections are

forged through understanding, compassion, and the simple joy of sharing stories with one another.

The Enchanted Treasure Hunt

A band of teenage explorers set out on a mission to locate the fabled Enchanted Treasure in a world of glistening rivers and majestic castles. It was stated that individuals who discovered this treasure could use its magical abilities to fulfil their greatest desires.

The group consisted of four friends: Emma, a brave and resourceful girl; Oliver, a clever and curious boy; Lily, a kind-hearted and observant girl; and Max, a loyal and adventurous boy. Together, they embarked on a thrilling treasure hunt that would test their courage and teamwork.

Their journey began in an ancient forest, where whispers of the treasure's whereabouts echoed among the trees. Guided by a mysterious map, the friends ventured deeper into the woods, encountering magical creatures and solving riddles along the way.

Their first challenge was presented by a mischievous gnome who guarded a hidden cave. He demanded a token of their friendship before revealing the path forward.

Recognizing the importance of unity, the friends clasped hands and vowed to support one another throughout their quest. Impressed by their loyalty, the gnome granted them access to the cave.

Inside the cave, a labyrinth of tunnels awaited them. Each passageway held a different obstacle—a rushing river, a room filled with riddles, and a chamber of mirrors that played tricks on their senses. With Emma's bravery, Oliver's intellect, Lily's empathy, and Max's determination, they overcame each challenge, inching closer to the treasure.

Finally, they reached the entrance of an ancient castle hidden atop a mountain. The castle's grand doors creaked open, revealing a majestic hall adorned with sparkling crystals. At the centre of the room stood a golden pedestal, upon which rested the coveted Enchanted Treasure.

However, just as they were about to claim their prize, a voice boomed through the hall. It belonged to the guardian of the treasure—a wise and ancient dragon named Aurelia. The dragon explained that the Enchanted Treasure could only be claimed by those who truly understood its power and would use it for the greater good.

Aurelia presented the friends with a final test—a series of moral dilemmas. They were challenged to make selfless choices, showing compassion and integrity in the face of temptation. Through heartfelt discussions and unwavering conviction, they proved their worthiness.

Impressed by their wisdom and noble hearts, Aurelia entrusted the Enchanted Treasure to the friends. With its magic, they vowed to bring joy, healing, and prosperity to their village and beyond.

As the friends returned home, their village celebrated their triumphant return. The Enchanted Treasure's powers were shared with the entire community, transforming lives and filling hearts with hope. Prosperity flourished, and kindness became a way of life.

Years later, the treasure hunt became a cherished tale passed down through generations—a reminder that true wealth lies not in material possessions but in the bonds of friendship, the strength of character, and the power of selflessness.

And so, the Enchanted Treasure remained a symbol of the remarkable adventure that taught Emma, Oliver , Lily, and Max that the greatest treasures

in life are found not in the pursuit of wealth, but in the journey of the heart.

The Incredible Flying Carpet

In a bustling marketplace of vibrant colours and enticing aromas, there stood a small rug merchant named Ali. Among his vast collection of carpets, there was one that held a secret—the Incredible Flying Carpet.

Legend had it that this magnificent carpet possessed the power to soar through the skies, carrying its passengers to faraway lands. Ali knew the tales well, but he had never seen the carpet take flight himself. One day, a young girl named Maya visited his shop.

Maya's eyes sparkled with curiosity as she gazed at the array of carpets, longing for adventure. Ali saw the same spirit of wonder in her eyes that he once had and decided to share the secret of the Incredible Flying Carpet with her.

Whispering the ancient incantation, Ali touched the carpet gently, and it began to stir.

The once-static threads transformed into a magical tapestry that shimmered with the promise of extraordinary journeys. Maya's excitement grew as she realized the possibilities before her.

Together, Ali and Maya climbed aboard the Incredible Flying Carpet. With a gentle command, it gracefully lifted off the ground, soaring into the boundless sky. Their hearts raced as they left the earth behind, witnessing the world from a whole new perspective.

The carpet took them to places they had only dreamed of—towering mountain peaks, lush rainforests, and sparkling oceans. They visited bustling marketplaces in far-off lands, where exotic spices filled the air and merchants traded tales as precious as gold.

As they travelled, Maya and Ali encountered people from different cultures and backgrounds, fostering deep connections and understanding. They learned about the beauty of diversity and the importance of empathy, realizing that despite their differences, humanity shared common hopes and dreams.

The Incredible Flying Carpet also allowed them to witness the wonders of nature up close. They marvelled at dazzling waterfalls, danced with dolphins in the crystal-clear waters, and stood in awe as the Aurora Borealis painted the sky with ethereal hues.

But with great adventure came great responsibility. Maya and Ali recognized the importance of preserving the beauty and sanctity of the places they visited. They made a pact to spread awareness about environmental conservation and to protect the natural wonders they had been privileged to witness.

As their journey came to an end, Maya and Ali returned to the bustling marketplace, their hearts brimming with gratitude and wisdom. The Incredible Flying Carpet settled gently on the ground, its magical powers temporarily dormant.

Maya thanked Ali for the incredible adventure and the life-changing lessons they had learned together. She promised to carry the spirit of their journey in her heart forever and to inspire others to embrace the beauty of exploration and the magic of the world.

With a final embrace, Maya bid Ali farewell, knowing that the Incredible Flying Carpet would choose another worthy soul to embark on its next remarkable voyage.

And so, the legend of the Incredible Flying Carpet continued, weaving its magic and carrying the dreams of those who sought the extraordinary.

Its tales would be told for generations to come, reminding all who listened that sometimes, the greatest adventures are found not in distant lands but within the courage to take flight and embrace the wonders of the world.

The Amazing Bubble Machine

Once upon a time, in a small town filled with wonder and joy, there lived a girl named Lily. Lily was a creative and curious girl, with a particular passion for soap bubbles. She loved watching bubbles float through the air, their vibrant colors sparkling in the sunlight.

Lily dreamed of creating the most amazing bubble experience for everyone in her town. One day, she stumbled upon an old and dusty box in her attic. Inside the box was a peculiar contraption—a Bubble Machine. It was a magical device that could produce bubbles of all shapes and sizes with a mere touch.

Excitement filled Lily's heart as she dusted off the machine and brought it to life. With a flick of a switch, the Bubble Machine hummed to life, and a stream of enchanting bubbles erupted from its nozzles. The air was soon filled with a kaleidoscope of shimmering spheres, much to Lily's delight.

News of Lily's Amazing Bubble Machine quickly spread throughout the town, drawing the attention of children and adults alike.

They gathered in the town square, eagerly waiting to witness the spectacle. As Lily stood before the crowd, she couldn't help but feel a mixture of nerves and excitement.

With a wave of her hand, she activated the Bubble Machine, and the magic began. Bubbles of all sizes, from tiny spheres to gigantic orbs, floated gracefully through the air. The townspeople gasped and cheered as they watched the bubbles dance, reflecting the colors of the rainbow.

Lily twirled and leapt, playfully interacting with the bubbles. She discovered that each bubble had its own unique personality. Some were mischievous, floating just out of reach, while others gently landed on outstretched hands, bringing smiles to the faces of those they touched.

The Bubble Machine seemed to have a mind of its own, creating astonishing bubble creations. There were bubble animals that seemed to come to life, bubble castles that sparkled with magical allure, and even bubble rainbows that stretched across the sky.

As the bubbles continued to mesmerize the townspeople, Lily realized that the true magic of the Amazing Bubble Machine was not just in the bubbles themselves, but in the joy and wonder they brought to those who experienced them. The bubbles had the power to ignite imaginations, uplift spirits, and bring people together in shared delight. The town was transformed into a whimsical wonderland as laughter and excitement filled the air. Children chase after bubbles, trying to catch them, while adults marvel at the ethereal beauty surrounding them. Time seemed to stand still as the community embraced the enchantment of the Amazing Bubble Machine.

As the sun began to set, casting a warm golden glow over the town, Lily knew that her mission was complete. The Amazing Bubble Machine had fulfilled its purpose—to spread joy and create unforgettable moments of happiness for everyone.

With a final flourish, Lily deactivated the Bubble Machine, allowing the last of the bubbles to gently pop and disappear. The crowd erupted in applause and cheers, expressing their gratitude for the extraordinary experience.

Lily's Amazing Bubble Machine became a cherished memory in the hearts of the townspeople. They would forever remember the magical moments they shared, and the bonds that were formed through the simple joy of bubbles.

And though the Bubble Machine eventually found its place back in the attic, gathering dust once more, the spirit of wonder and the joy it brought remained alive in the town. It became a symbol of the power of imagination, reminding everyone that sometimes, the most incredible moments can be found in the simplest of things.

Since that time, the community has conducted an annual event called the Bubble Festival where kids and adults may come together to make their own wonderful moments using bubble wands.

The Brave Princess and the Dragon's Quest

Once upon a time, in a kingdom far away, there lived a brave princess named Amelia. Unlike the other princesses in neighboring kingdoms who spent their days attending royal balls and receiving suitors, Amelia had a spirit of adventure that burned within her.

One day, as Amelia wandered through the royal library, she stumbled upon an ancient book that spoke of a great dragon's quest. It told of a fearsome dragon that had terrorized the land for centuries, hoarding a treasure beyond imagination deep within its lair.

Amelia's heart fluttered with excitement as she read the tales of brave knights who had attempted to vanquish the dragon but failed. Determined to prove herself, Amelia decided to embark on this perilous quest.

With her trusted steed, Storm, and her loyal companion, a wise old owl named Oliver, Amelia set out on her journey. The kingdom watched in awe as their brave princess rode forth, her golden armor shining in the sun.

Through treacherous forests and over towering mountains, Amelia followed the clues from the ancient book. She encountered dangerous creatures, navigated treacherous ravines, and weathered fierce storms. But with each obstacle she faced, her determination only grew stronger.

Finally, after weeks of relentless pursuit, Amelia reached the entrance to the dragon's lair. The ground trembled beneath her as she took a deep breath and entered the dark cavern.

Inside, she discovered a vast chamber adorned with glittering gold, sparkling jewels, and magnificent treasures. And there, coiled protectively around the treasure, was the dragon—a majestic creature with scales as dark as the night sky.

Amelia approached the dragon with respect and spoke with a steady voice, explaining her purpose. Surprisingly, the dragon listened attentively, its piercing eyes filled with a mix of curiosity and wisdom. It revealed that the treasure it guarded was not meant to be hoarded but to be shared with those who showed true courage and compassion.

Moved by Amelia's bravery and noble intentions, the dragon presented her with a golden key—a key that unlocked not just the treasure, but also the

hearts of the people. It spoke of a world where kindness and empathy reigned, a world that Amelia had the power to bring to life.

With the key in hand, Amelia returned to the kingdom, her heart full of hope. She called upon the people to come together, to unite in a mission of compassion and understanding. The citizens, inspired by their brave princess, embraced her vision wholeheartedly.

Under Amelia's guidance, the kingdom flourished. People set aside their differences and worked together to build a better society. Acts of kindness became the norm, and the kingdom became a beacon of harmony and joy.

Years passed, and Amelia's legacy lived on. The dragon's quest had transformed her into a true leader, admired and respected by all. The kingdom thrived under her wise rule, and stories of her bravery and the dragon's quest were passed down from generation to generation.

Amelia, a courageous princess, demonstrated that real strength comes from the capacity for empathy and compassion as well as from the conviction that each person had the capacity to affect positive change in the world.

As the kingdom basked in the light of unity and love, they celebrated the brave princess who had embarked on the Dragon's Quest and emerged victorious, forever etching her name in the annals of their history.

The Magical Forest Friends

Once upon a time, nestled deep within an enchanted forest, there existed a magical world filled with wonder and beauty. In this mystical realm, the trees whispered secrets, the flowers sang melodies, and the animals possessed extraordinary powers.

In the heart of the forest, there lived four special friends: Oliver the wise owl, Luna the graceful deer, Milo the mischievous squirrel, and Ruby the playful fox. Each possessed a unique gift bestowed upon them by the enchanting spirits of the forest.

Oliver, with his keen intellect and ancient wisdom, was known as the sage of the woods. He guided the others with his insightful advice and kept the forest creatures safe with his sharp eyes.

Luna, adorned with majestic antlers that shimmered in the moonlight, possessed the ability to heal wounded animals and bring harmony to the forest. Her gentle presence and soothing touch brought comfort to all who sought her help.

Milo, with his agile movements and quick wit, could communicate with the trees and plants, coaxing them to grow and flourish. He used his powers to create luscious groves and vibrant meadows, ensuring the forest was always teeming with life.

Ruby, with her fiery red fur and boundless energy, could harness the power of the elements. She could summon gusts of wind, conjure droplets of rain, and even create small bursts of light, adding a touch of magic to the forest.

Together, these four friends protected and nurtured the enchanted forest, forming an unbreakable bond. They explored every nook and cranny, uncovering the hidden wonders of their home. The forest creatures, from the tiny fairies to the gentle giants, regarded them with admiration and respect.

One day, as the friends ventured deeper into the forest, they discovered a small wounded bird. Its wing was injured, preventing it from soaring through the sky. Filled with compassion, Luna gently approached the bird, her healing touch mending its injured wing. The bird chirped with delight, expressing its gratitude.

Impressed by the friends' kindness, the bird revealed a secret. It spoke of an ancient prophecy that foretold the arrival of a great darkness that threatened to consume the forest. The friends listened intently, realizing that their powers and unity were needed now more than ever.

Driven by their sense of duty, the Magical Forest Friends embarked on a quest to protect their home from the encroaching darkness. They traversed treacherous terrains and faced formidable challenges, using their unique abilities to overcome each obstacle.

Along the way, they encountered a variety of forest creatures who joined their cause, including wise old turtles, mischievous sprites, and graceful butterflies. Together, they formed an alliance, determined to preserve the enchantment and beauty of the forest.

As they neared their final destination, the friends stood before the source of the darkness—a twisted, gnarled tree surrounded by an aura of malevolence. With their powers combined, they unleashed a surge of energy, purifying the darkness and restoring balance to the forest.

The enchanted forest rejoiced, as nature celebrated the victory of light over darkness. The friends were hailed as heroes, their names whispered in gratitude by every leaf and every blade of grass.

From that day forward, the Magical Forest Friends continued to protect and nurture their beloved home. They ensured that harmony and magic thrived, allowing the forest to be a sanctuary for all creatures, great and small.

And so, the tale of the Magical Forest Friends spread far and wide, becoming a legend passed down through generations. Even today, if you listen closely, you might hear the whispers of their names on the wind, a reminder of the enduring power of friendship, courage, and the magic that resides within the heart of the forest.

THE MAGICAL STORY CHEST

As we bid farewell to "The Magical Story Chest: A Collection of Enchanting Adventures," we carry with us the echoes of laughter, the warmth of cherished memories, and the spark of boundless imagination. We hope these tales have transported you to worlds where magic dances on every page and dreams take flight. Thank you, dear reader, for embarking on this extraordinary journey with us. May these enchanting adventures continue to ignite your imagination, inspire your own stories, and remind you that within the realms of the written word, wonders await. Keep exploring, keep dreaming, and may the magic of storytelling forever illuminate your path. Farewell, and may your own story be filled with joy and enchantment.